D0559183

More Than Enough

By
Rod Parsley

More Than Enough

By
Rod Parsley

RESULTS
PUBLISHING

More Than Enough

ISBN 1-933336-86-2

By Rod Parsley
Published by Results Publishing
World Harvest Church
PO Box 32932
Columbus, OH 43232-0932, USA
www.rodparsley.com

TABLE OF CONTENTS

INTRODUCTION

Years before a contemporary television program became popular by portraying celebrities' homes, there was another program that featured the lifestyles of fabulously rich and famous people. Fascination with wealth and all that it provides is nothing new, but it inevitably produces this question: "Where do they get all that money?"

The answer is that it is already in the earth.

Don't believe the lie that there is not enough. There is more than enough for you, for me, and for others as well. Our God is extravagant—He is a God of more than enough, and He wants you to have not just enough, but more than enough to accomplish His will.

The biggest difference between you and someone who has more than you is knowledge. This book will help you close the knowledge gap and go from not enough to *More Than Enough*.

— Rod Parsley

We were created for the conflict,
formed for the fight,
and built for the battle.

CHAPTER ONE
ENOUGH IS ENOUGH

The man labored until it felt as though his back was breaking. He had long since stopped trying to keep the sweat from running down his brow and stinging his eyes. Day after day he had worked in the pitiless Palestinian heat, doing his best to make sure this crop would be enough to feed his family. And here came his enemies again—just like the year before and the year before that. The thieves had come to steal his lentils and leave him and his family hungry for another year.

Lentils are small and often overlooked as a food item here in America. They are overshadowed by other grain crops that are more familiar and widespread in the New World. But for millions in other countries, they are a staple that means the difference between satisfaction and starvation. They were important enough to be a factor in two Biblical controversies.

Lentil soup was what persuaded Esau to sell his birthright to Jacob. His price in his pride and selfishness was nothing more than a chunk of bread and a bowl of soup. But lentils also find a place in another narrative that has to do with you, your seed, and your harvest. It's found in 2 Samuel 23: 11-12:

> And after him was Shammah the son of Agee the Hararite. And the Philistines were gathered together into a troop, where was a piece of ground full of lentils: and the people fled from the Philistines. But he stood in the midst of the ground, and defended it, and slew the Philistines: and the Lord wrought a great victory.

Ancient Israel was a nation of farmers. The vast majority of people were either involved in agriculture directly or indirectly. Even in David's time, when a standing army of professional warriors was mobilized, many of the men still had their own property and continued to raise crops on them. Shammah was such a man.

If you happen to be a property owner, then you know how important it is to be very interested in what is happening on your land or in your house. You are the one who pays the taxes, performs the labor, and takes the risks, so you have a vested interest in everything that happens there. You are willing to do things for your land that you would not do for any other parcel of ground.

This is a key that helps us understand Shammah's behavior compared to everyone else who fled when the Philistines arrived. I believe the thing that made him stand and fight when his comrades ran away was that he was not just defending someone else's property—he was standing on his own ground.

As you remember, land was assigned to tribes in the days of Joshua by lot. Each male head of his household received a portion of land within his tribe's allotment so he could earn a living and have a place to raise his family. These lands were passed down through many generations, and were continually improved and developed to be as productive as possible. Digging wells, erecting buildings, establishing vineyards, and planting crops was done by hand,

and was difficult, labor-intensive work. Land-owners were justifiably proud of productive cropland, vineyards, or orchards.

During times of invasion or other disturbances, enemies would destroy the productive capability of the land by doing things such as stopping up wells, cutting down trees, and even sowing the land with salt so that any efforts at farming would be compromised for years and even for generations. Sometimes, enemy forces would allow the Israelites to do all the work of planting and maintaining the crops, then steal the fruit of their labor at harvest time.

This amounted to the children of Israel providing slave labor for their oppressors, where they did all the work but got none of the benefit.

Everything the adversary did was to minimize the ability of the landowner to plant a seed and reap a harvest, which struck at the very core of Israel's economy and the landowner's livelihood. Who knows how many times the Philistines, the implacable enemies of Israel, had come upon Shammah's land just as his lentils were ready for harvest and stole them right out from under him? In this state of affairs, Shammah was no better off than his ancestors living under the taskmaster's lash in Egypt. In fact, it was worse, because in Egypt at least they knew they were slaves. Here in Israel, Shammah thought he was free, but the Philistines came to take that upon which they had wrought no labor, in essence making him their slave.

Think about the irony of it. Shammah was the one who had to clear the land. He uprooted trees and shrubs and cut down weeds. He dug up rocks and stones and hauled them to the edges of the field. Then he had to plow the land with a reluctant donkey and a wooden plow with a single point. Then he had to furrow the field and sow his seed. Then he had to hoe out the weeds that tried to strangle his young plants from flourishing. He had to drive away the birds and the other creatures that wanted a free meal. He had to trust that rain would fall in the right amounts at the right times. He had to guard against crop destroying pests and hope that his plants would not fall prey to a host of diseases that could wipe him out. All this went on for months at a time, and only after all this work was a crop ready to harvest.

Then the enemy would show up and claim the crop for themselves. Instead of Shammah feeding his children, he would work all year only to hand it over to his adversaries, who would use it to feed their children.

But this year was different. Shammah asked his friends and neighbors to help him defend his property from the marauding Philistines. At the appointed day they were all there, and sure enough, they saw the dust of an approaching wagon train in the distance. Shammah's enemies were showing up right on schedule. Shammah stood in the middle of his field and let them come. As they rattled and clanked up to the border of his land, it seemed like there were more of them than usual. They stopped and observed him scornfully.

Finally, their leader spoke up. "We've come for our lentils, farmer. We hope you've got a good crop for us. Again." All the Philistines began to laugh. "Step aside, Israelite, and we'll take what is ours."

Shammah was determined to stand up to these thieves. He shouted, "Enough is enough! I am not going to stand by and watch you take the fruits of my labor one more time!"

The Philistine snarled, "How do you propose to stop us?"

Shammah said, "My friends and I will fight you for this field."

The Philistine replied, "Friends? You must be pretty unpopular, Israelite. I don't see your friends." With this, the entire Philistine troop began to laugh louder than ever.

Shammah looked around, and was astonished to discover that all those he thought were standing with him had abandoned him. He was alone against an entire company of Philistines who would kill him if necessary to strip his fields of every last lentil he had grown. A voice in his head told him that it wasn't worth it—he could grow another crop next year. Maybe by that time things would be different. His knees began to give way. He felt his back beginning to bow and he was about to turn around and run in defeat.

Then Shammah remembered something that he hadn't thought of before. He remembered how he had gone to the cave Adullam when David was there in exile from King Saul. He remembered the stories of the exploits of David and a small band of men that gathered around him that had determined to see the yoke of Philistine bondage broken from the lives of all those who lived in Israel. He thought of the tales of the lion and the bear, and how the Philistine champion, Goliath, fell at the blow of a smooth stone from the sling of a shepherd boy. He heard again the songs of how David and his men fought impossible odds time after time, and were always delivered by the God of Israel.

With a start he remembered that he was not just a farmer waiting to be victimized by his enemies, he was one of those men whose hearts had been knit to David through those many months of trial. He had forgotten in the midst of his farming efforts that he had been in the cave with a giant killer, and if David could prevail over the Philistines, he could, too. He realized that he knew not just how to handle a hoe, but he had also learned how to handle a sword. In fact, he had girded his sword to his belt before coming to his field.

All these thoughts went through Shammah's mind in a moment as he faced the Philistine mob while they were still laughing at him. They said, "Who do you think you are, little man? What makes you think an Israelite farmer can beat the Philistine army? Step aside, before we cut you down where you stand!"

And then the most curious thing happened to Shammah. He thought about it many times afterward, and never really understood what it was. The best way he could describe it was as if something came up from the ground, through his feet and legs and all the way out the top of his head. He felt energized and strengthened in a way he never had before. It was even more dramatic than how he felt when he had fought with his comrades around him on every side. He was not afraid, because he was not alone.

The Philistines asked him who he was. He would tell them. He took a step forward and stuck his hoe in the ground as though it were a javelin. He shouted with a voice that reverberated off the mountains on either side, "I am Shammah!" Then he drew his sword.

Shammah was surrounded, but he began fighting as though his sword had a mind of its own. Every time his blade flashed a Philistine went down. His enemies soon discovered that even though the farmer was vastly outnumbered, he was outfighting them. They began to think of reasons they should not sacrifice their lives as so many of their fellows had done for a few wagons full of lentils. Before long their fight turned into a full fledged rout. They were convinced that something besides an angry farmer was opposing them, and they turned their wagons around and ran like a pack of whipped curs, never to return.

When Shammah announced his name, he was not just telling his enemies who he was. He was telling them that the Lord of hosts, the God of battles, had come to defend that field. Jehovah-Shammah means the Lord is there, personally present in the situation. The Philistines thought they were fighting with a farmer. They didn't realize they were coming against the God of Israel. This was the same God who manifested Himself in the temple of the Philistine fish god Dagon in such a way that Dagon was toppled from his seat, eventually breaking off his hands and head. When Shammah shouted his name, the true and living God showed up to defend His people and His land, and no Philistine idolater could stand before Him.

Shammah could have stayed home that day and not gone out to his field. The Philistines would have stripped his crop bare and laughed about it all the way back to their cities. But Shammah did something that far too few in the body of Christ are willing to do—he fought. This should not seem so strange to us; after all, the apostle Paul told us that we would need to put on the armor of God for the battles we would fight (see Ephesians 6). I like to say it this way—your armor prophesies a battle. Instead of shrinking back from the conflict, we should run to the fight, because our God has anointed us to fight and to win. He is called the Lord of hosts, the God of battles, and He has never lost a fight.

We need to settle this in our hearts: we were created for the conflict, formed for the fight, and built for the battle. Great victories are the result of great battles. We cannot win if we do not fight. There is no middle ground. You cannot negotiate with your adversary, or find a position of compromise with him. The Bible says the devil's purpose is to steal, to kill, and to destroy, and if it is possible he will do it by maneuvering you into giving up without a fight. He knows that if you resist him, you will have supernatural help that is insurmountable by the forces of hell. When you stand against your adversary, you never stand alone, and you are never at a disadvantage, even though it may look like you are surrounded and outnumbered.

Here is a scriptural example. In 2 Kings, chapter six, the Syrian army surrounded the city of Dothan with the aim of capturing the prophet Elisha. Elisha's servant went out early in the morning and saw the Syrian host encompassing the entire city. The man was filled with fear. When he reported what he saw to the prophet, Elisha was untroubled. He responded, "Fear not: for they that be with us are more than they that be with them." Elisha asked God to let his servant see what was happening in the spiritual realm as well as in the natural realm. There were horses and chariots of fire all around Elisha. Neither the prophet nor his servant was in danger from the enemy army.

Malachi chapter three is often used as a text dealing with tithes and offerings. But there are some truths contained in verse 11 that I need to mention regarding God's defense of His people. It says,

> And I will rebuke the devourer for your
> sakes, and he shall not destroy the fruits
> of your ground; neither shall your vine
> cast her fruit before the time in the field,
> saith the Lord of hosts.

The words "ground" and "field" speak of
places where you sow your seed. God is interested in your harvest, and He watches over the
ground where you sow your seed. Of course, we
need to know which ground is good ground.
Good ground is a place that produces an abundant crop of what is sown. In the parable of the
sower in Mark chapter four, Jesus identified different kinds of ground, and only one of four
seed beds actually produced the desired harvest.
We need to take note of where we are sowing
and make sure that our seed is falling on productive soil.

The best soil is that which produces the best
fruit. The signs of a productive church are
found in Mark chapter 16, verse 17-18:

> And these signs shall follow them that
> believe; in my name they shall cast out
> devils; they shall speak with new

tongues; they shall take up serpents; and if they drink any deadly thing, it shall not hurt them; they shall lay hands on the sick, and they shall recover.

When you find soil that is producing this kind of harvest; that is where you should sow your seed. If you have been sowing your seed in soil that is not producing these things, you will not get much of a harvest regardless of how much seed you sow.

After your seed is sown, the thief will come to try to stop it from growing to maturity. Malachi 3:11 calls him the devourer. The word "devourer" literally means "seed eater." But in this verse God said He would do something about the devourer, or seed eater, who comes to stop your harvest. He said He would rebuke him.

Now it's one thing for you to rebuke someone, but it is another thing altogether for God to rebuke someone. The word rebuke means "Stop it! That's enough!"

God Himself said that if you would plant your seed—your tithes and offerings—in the fertile soil of a productive storehouse, or local church, that He would see to it that the seed eater was rebuked. As with Shammah, God will stand with you at the border of your field and tell the adversary, "Stop it! That's enough!" That's enough stealing. That's enough robbing. That's enough sickness. That's enough pain. No more broken relationships. No more poor financial decision making. No more foreclosures or bankruptcies.

Not only will God watch over your seed, He will continue to protect it so that it grows and flourishes into an abundant harvest for you and your household. Nothing you have sown will miscarry or fail to produce what is necessary for you to accomplish God's purpose.

Sow your seed in your fertile field and stand. Refuse to give in to the forces of deception and intimidation that try to move you away from expecting and reaping your harvest. You are not standing alone. The Lord of hosts, the God of battles, stands with you to defend your seed and your field. Regardless of how perilous the times or grave the circumstances, the Lord will defend you, your seed, your harvest, and your house from every strategy of the devourer.

...Holy, holy, holy,
is the Lord of hosts:
the whole earth is full of His glory.
~Isaiah 6:3

CHAPTER TWO
WHAT IS HIS IS HOLY

Two men were summoned to appear before the king. One had been there before; the other one had never had such an experience. The neophyte had sense enough to know he could not act as he pleased when before royalty, so he asked the veteran what protocols he should observe. "Treat him with the utmost respect," came the answer. "And if he asks you for anything—your opinion, your service, or your house—give it to him. Remember, he is the king."

In the past, kings ruled with such absolute authority that subjects who approached them customarily included some phrase in their salutation that represented their respect for the ruling monarch. "Live for ever" is one of these—a short step from regarding the royalty as divine. In some cultures, divinity was automatically accorded to rulers, even though their actions betrayed their humanity all too frequently. In any case, ancient kingdoms did little to dispel the notion that their rulers were divine, and ruled by divine right.

Unlike so many other kingdoms, Israel did have a divine king—none other than God Himself. In contrast to the customs and whims of earthly kings, God set out in writing what He claimed as His own—and it never changed. He put down the guidelines for offering first fruits to Him in Deuteronomy chapter 26. Verses 13 through 15 relate some of what the worshipper was to rehearse before the Lord: "…I have brought away the hallowed things out of mine house…neither have I taken away ought thereof for any unclean use…."

From the very earliest chapters of human history, God made it clear that what was His was holy. It was not to be trifled with or trivialized by men. Jesus reinforced this concept when He taught His disciples to pray. The very first words of His model prayer emphasized God's holiness. You may remember the words: "Our Father which art in heaven, hallowed be thy name…."

Hallowed, of course, means holy. This is a primary characteristic of the God we serve. When Isaiah saw God's glory as recorded in chapter six of his book, verse three says that the angels who stand watch at the doorposts of the temple repeat this aspect of God's nature continually: "...Holy, holy, holy, is the Lord of hosts: the whole earth is full of His glory." God's name is holy. They didn't whisper it, either—Isaiah said the pillars of the temple were moved at the sound.

The holiness of God has been such a fixture in Jewish tradition that they avoid saying His name or even writing it to avoid the possibility of taking that name in vain. God's name represents all He is and all He has. If He is holy, what belongs to Him is holy as well.

When we think in terms of material possessions, we don't include God in our deliberations. After all, God is a spirit, and He doesn't need earthly things to get along in heaven. But this is a narrow view. God is really the owner of everything, since He made all of it. We try to persuade ourselves that our lives are uniquely ours to do with as we wish, but that is a tragic mistake. We will eventually have to answer to God for everything we have done. We are only the stewards, or managers, of the things that come into our possession for the brief time we spend on earth, and we will have to give an account of our stewardship to the God who really owns it all.

Our failure to see this concept clearly is why so many people are shocked when they read passages such as Malachi 3: 8-9:

> Will a man rob God? Yet ye have robbed me. But ye say, wherein have we robbed thee? In tithes and offerings. Ye are cursed with a curse: for ye have robbed me, even this whole nation.

I have seen people recoil in horror when I have read this passage in public meetings. I can see the wheels turning in their heads as they try to justify their actions in light of what the Word of God says. God very boldly declares some to be thieves and robbers—and sometimes the very ones He accuses are sitting on church pews on Sunday morning.

It's really not a hard concept. You remember hearing lectures about it when you were in elementary school. "If you take something that doesn't belong to you without permission, what is that called? That's right, boys and girls, that's called stealing. We should never, ever take something that belongs to someone else, because that's not right." We didn't realize it, but the notions of the importance of personal property rights and the fundamental differences between right and wrong were placed in us when we were very young.

Why we do things that are not right and take what does not belong to us goes back as far as the garden of Eden in Genesis chapter three. There, in the midst of the garden, God planted a tree and told Adam not to eat of it, for he would surely die if he did so. This was a test of obedience and of love. Adam had access to everything God created, except the one thing God reserved for Himself. It was not beyond the ordinary for God to have something of His own there in the middle of the paradise He created—after all, He made it, and Adam would have had none of it if God had not given it to him.

We don't know how long Adam and his wife enjoyed the fellowship of God's presence and of one another there in that perfect world. The most fanciful flights of human imagination have never come close to recreating the atmosphere that must have existed in Eden as God and man walked together in harmony every day. Adam and his bride enjoyed what was theirs, which was everything God had made—except for one thing.

The tree of the knowledge of good and evil must have been honored, since it was in the midst of the garden—very likely a place of prominence. It was acknowledged, but not partaken of, since it belonged to God. It was not the same as the other trees—indeed, not the same as anything else God made, since it was appropriated as His personal possession by His divine decree. God exercised His right of dominion over that tree in a way that exceeded all else in creation. It was set apart—it was holy—it was *other*. Even though it was a tree in the sense that all other trees were made in a similar fashion, the thing that set it apart was not the fruit that it bore or its location in the garden. The thing that truly set it apart from all others was the decree that God placed upon the tree and the restriction that God placed upon Adam and his household.

For Adam and his wife to partake of something that God said was forbidden would be to make themselves greater than God. God is and has every right to expect to be regarded as first by the things that He has created. The violation of what He said was His was an offense that made Him lower than His creation, and such a violation could not be without consequence. In this case, since Adam and Eve refused to remain separated *to* God in holiness, they became separated *from* God in their unholy act of rebellion.

Sin opened the door to death and disorder. Man was banished from the garden to the sterile plains east of Eden. Instead of blossom there was dust; instead of growth, there was decline; decay replaced flourishing. All of creation fell into turmoil as a result of disobedience. We have suffered its effects from then until now, and we still wait for final liberation from the curse.

In those days, there was a tree in the middle of the garden. Today our stone of offense is something different, yet the principle is still the same. The grace of God is extended to us in redemption, including eternal life for our spirit, salvation for our soul, and healing for our body. In addition, God did not forget that we live in a material world, and He promised to bless us with all we would need or desire to accomplish His will.

Jesus very simply and eloquently elaborated on God's care for us by giving us examples such as birds and flowers. Our heavenly Father is more concerned about us than He is the fowls of the air or the flowers of the field. As with Adam,

God has richly given us all things to enjoy. But as with Adam, there is a solitary restriction. It stands in the middle of our existence just as the tree stood in the midst of the garden, and once again, we hear the voice of God saying, "Don't partake of it—if you do, death will be the result."

Our tree is the tithe.

What is it about humanity that causes the forbidden thing to seem more attractive? Just as surely as you tell a child not to touch a thing, they crave it more than ever. I have known people who have met with all manner of catastrophe because of their own actions, and they were honest enough to stop trying to rationalize their behavior. "I do it because I want to," they say, even though they fully recognize that their carnal desires lead to calamity and distress.

God said, "That's mine. Don't eat of it—don't use it—leave it to Me." And for a while we do not eat of it. Then we begin to bargain with ourselves and try to convince ourselves that God didn't really mean what He said. The more we look at what is forbidden, the more we are tempted, and after all, every man has his price. Eventually we yield, and death comes. It may come in an unfamiliar form, but death will ultimately be the result of forsaking the command of God and violating His holiness by our disobedience.

This brings greater understanding to the terms used in Deuteronomy 26. The worshipper was instructed to say, "I have brought away the hallowed things out of my house...." What made the things hallowed? It wasn't anything the worshipper did that made the thing holy—he only responded to something God had already done. God put His hand upon it, and that made it holy. The only rational response of the worshipper in that case was to agree with God's decree and give it to Him wholly and completely.

Further, the Bible says, "...neither have I taken away ought thereof for any unclean use...." Again, what would make a hallowed or sanctified thing unclean? Using it for anything other than that for which it was sanctified would cause it to be unholy and unfit for an offering to a holy God.

God was trying to train His people—in ways they would surely understand—that He was holy, therefore the things that He claimed were also holy. When a sacrifice was brought to Him, it must be the first and the best—otherwise, He would be regarded as less than He was. If His people truly saw Him as a holy God, they would offer Him their best. If they did less, it did not make Him less, but it showed that the worshippers did not regard Him as first and best. They were either holding something better back for themselves, making themselves gods, or they were acknowledging that someone or something else was more important to them than the God who gave them life. Either way, God was relegated to second place, and He deserves better. After all, He is God.

Certainly this idea is not hard for us to understand. When I was young, and someone planned to be with us for dinner but was unable to join us in time for the meal, my parents would inevitably set some of the best of the meal aside for them so they could eat when they arrived. It was always more than they actually could eat, but it was reserved for them. To touch it was regarded as a very serious offense in my household. It was sanctified for a specific purpose.

If we will do this much for an earthly visitor, how much more should we set apart for God's use what He asks of us? To touch it should be regarded as a very serious offense, because it has already been designated as belonging to another. To use it for any other purpose would be unclean, or unholy. It could rightly be regarded as stealing.

God said to Israel, "You have robbed Me." What did they take from Him? They took for their own use that which God said belonged to Him. He didn't object to their use of the tithe because He would starve if they withheld it. He became indignant because they said He was in first place, but their actions betrayed them.

Through their disobedience, God also lost His opportunity to bless and increase their harvest when He had every intention of doing so.

Stewardship cannot be counterfeited—the checkbook register may be out of balance, but it tells no lies. If someone says they love God supremely, their lives—all of their lives, not just parts of them—will tell the tale. We cannot love God first and foremost and withhold from Him what He requires. God Himself calls them who do thieves and robbers.

When bank robbers are apprehended, the authorities don't let them keep all the things they acquire with the money they have stolen. They must make restitution, and then suffer additional consequences as well.

We regularly hear of the misguided exploits of would-be thieves who do something so dramatically stupid it results in their swift apprehension. Reports of these escapades leave us shaking our heads wondering why anyone would even attempt such things. But I would counter that the ultimate in ignorance is to try to rob God with impunity. Why would anyone do such a thing? Those who try to rob God may feel that since He is merciful, He will not try to exact any retribution.

This attitude has led to a general lack of respect for the name of God, even among those who ought to respect Him most. God is merciful, and it is His mercy that has preserved many in the church despite their disregard for His holiness. When Ananias and his wife Sapphira lied to the Holy Ghost about their offering, the judgment of God came upon them swiftly and surely, and everyone present knew their fault was a lethal one. It not only caused great respect for God's name in the church, but also in the community. Surely people took great care after that to make sure they gave God the respect He deserved. They withheld nothing from Him that He required of them.

How different is the case today! Not only is God's name held in contempt in the world, but He is not even regarded as holy by many in the church. How do we know this? His own people do not even respect the tithe—they treat as common the things God says are holy.

I am not advocating that God strike people with immediate judgment if they fail to offer a prompt payment of their tithe. God doesn't catch those stealing from Him and put them in prison, but He does allow the consequences of their disobedience to catch up with them. I have seen the suffering that results in people offending God's holiness by taking what belongs to Him and using it for other things. This suffering manifests itself in financial struggles that could have been avoided if first things were really first. Unfortunately, when this happens many people feel that God is to blame for their lack, rather than acknowledging that they are the victims of their own bad decisions.

New Testament believers should not have to wait, as Belshazzar did, for handwriting to appear on the wall telling them they are weighed in the balance and found wanting. It is not just our checkbooks that are out of balance in these situations, it is our lives that need balancing.

The Bible says an unjust balance is an abomination to the Lord. If we put everything on our side of the scale and nothing on God's side, our entire lives will be an offense to God.

Belshazzar was the king of the mighty Babylonian empire. From a material standpoint, he had everything that a person could ever desire. But even though his treasuries were full, his life was empty. He was found wanting.

We can have every material blessing and still be empty of the blessing of God. Our offices, our homes, and our lives can be overflowing with physical things, and our relationships, our minds, and our hearts can be void of the life that only comes from knowing and loving God and responding to Him appropriately.

Listen to Jesus' warning to the Laodicean church in Revelation chapter 3, verses 17-19:

> Because thou sayest, I am rich, and increased with goods, and have need of nothing; and knowest not that thou art wretched, and miserable, and poor, and blind, and naked: I counsel thee to buy of me gold tried in the fire, that thou

mayest be rich; and white raiment, that thou mayest be clothed, and that the shame of thy nakedness do not appear; and anoint thine eyes with eyesalve, that thou mayest see. As many as I love, I rebuke and chasen: be zealous therefore, and repent.

Have you been acknowledging God's holiness by giving Him what is His? If not, I encourage you to be zealous about repentance so you can receive the blessing of the King.

When a word from God is given,
reason is never required—
faith and faith alone must answer
the door.

CHAPTER THREE
THE STRANGER AT THE GATE

It had been more than three years since the last rain. She and her son had managed to survive, but the woman wondered if they really were the lucky ones. As she trudged through the dust toward the city gate to look for some sticks to make a fire, it seemed to her the end was surely near.

She was startled by the appearance of the stranger. She was sure she had never seen him before, and she wondered how he could have traveled very far in the heat. She was even more surprised at his request for a drink. Where had he been living for the past three years that he didn't know about the drought and famine? But the laws of hospitality were as much a part of her as her bones. The cistern beneath her house still held a cupful of water. As she turned away to do his bidding, he asked for something to eat. She explained to this impertinent stranger as respectfully as she could that she would have to give him her last meal. He did not relent, but told her there would be enough for all of them. She thought he was crazy, but since they would all perish soon anyway, she would do what he asked. She had no idea of the miracle that was about to be set in motion.

The stranger was Elijah the prophet, and the drought and subsequent famine was the one he predicted as a result of the idolatry of Ahab and Jezebel. (See 1 Kings, chapter 17.) While the rest of the country suffered, Elijah was kept safe and well fed at a place near the brook Cherith where the water continued to flow, and ravens brought him bread and flesh every morning and evening. He was literally hidden there from the devastation that was going on all around him. But as it turned out, it was only temporary.

Eventually the brook dried up, and Elijah knew that change was imminent. Times of transition and seasons of change are not always comfortable or easy, but they are necessary. Elijah enjoyed abundant provision in his country hideaway, but even that water supply went dry and the ravens seemed to forget the address. He had to move or perish. But where should he go?

We can easily become such creatures of habit that we resist any sort of change. We tend to establish routines that repeat the easiest ways of doing things, and don't want to deal with any disruptions. But our lives with God are not individual events, but rather a process. In order for God to get us to our destination, He sometimes has to make it uncomfortable in our present circumstances—otherwise we would never implement any kind of change at all. In other words, loss is the first step toward change. Elijah became very accustomed to his condition at the brook, but God had something else in mind for him, and so He arranged to move Elijah to the next step in His purpose.

Don't panic when you notice things that used to sustain you start drying up. When the company downsizes or the factory closes, don't give in to despair—those things are not your true source anyway. God will sustain you, but you need to hear what He is saying to you during a time of transition. When the brook dried up and it was time for Elijah to move, the word of the Lord came to him. The word of the Lord will come to you as well, if you will listen for it.

God told Elijah to go to the city of Zarephath, near the city of Zidon (Sidon). But that wasn't all—God told Elijah that He had commanded a widow to sustain him there.

This was unusual for two reasons. One was that Zarephath was a city just beyond the historic border of Israel, and those who lived there may not have been particularly friendly toward Elijah or his God. Another is that God told Elijah that a widow would sustain him. Widows were traditionally one of the groups at the bottom of the economic scale, since in most cases the wage earner was the man of the house, and if he was dead, his wife had no means of making a living. Nevertheless, the word of God was sure, and Elijah proceeded to Zarephath as he was told. If he had gone anywhere else, he would have suffered and probably starved. God didn't tell him to go anywhere else, because

Elijah's provision was only in the place God prescribed.

This point was borne out by Jesus in Luke:

> But I tell you of a truth, many widows were in Israel in the days of Elias, when the heaven was shut up three years and six months, when great famine was throughout all the land; but unto none of them was Elias sent, save unto Sarepta, a city of Sidon, unto a woman that was a widow (4:25-26)

Why this widow instead of the thousands of others who were suffering and dying throughout the country? What made her different? What was it about her that attracted God's attention?

Smith Wigglesworth, that great English apostle of faith, put it this way: "There is something about faith that will cause God to pass over a thousand people just to get to you." Second Chronicles 16:9 says,

> For the eyes of the Lord run to and fro throughout the whole earth, to shew Himself strong in the behalf of them whose heart is perfect toward Him...

I believe that what distinguished this widow of Zarephath was that she was willing to receive the word of the Lord through His prophet when nobody else would have. It took a great deal of faith to give away what looked like the last morsel of bread and the last drink of water to someone she didn't know and had never met before. Keep in mind this was before Elijah had made a name for himself in all Israel by overcoming the prophets of Baal on Mount Carmel or calling fire down from heaven. It is unlikely this woman had ever so much as heard his name.

Yet she did as Elijah asked, even though it could have meant death for herself and her son. He did not ask her for what she did not have, but for what she certainly must have wanted to keep for herself. She had no assurances as she turned away from the city gate and started for home to bake a morsel of bread for the visitor. He did not identify himself to her by name or sign or token. It was only after she was already on her way that Elijah gave her this word:

> For thus saith the Lord God of Israel, the barrel of meal shall not waste, neither shall the cruse of oil fail, until the day that the Lord sendeth rain upon the earth (1 Kings 17:14).

Let me give you the last two verses of this:

> And she went and did according to the saying of Elijah: and she, and he, and her house, did eat many days. And the barrel of meal wasted not, neither did the cruse of oil fail, according to the word of the Lord, which he spake by Elijah (1 Kings 17:15-16).

First, the Bible says she did according to the saying of Elijah. But then it goes on to say the miracle of provision came to pass according to the word of the Lord, which He spoke through Elijah. So which was it—Elijah's word or God's word?

The fact is, Elijah only told the woman what God commanded him to speak. In essence, his word to her was God's word. The remarkable thing about this woman was that she did not wait to hear from God directly—she received the word of the prophet as though it was a word from God. When she acted according to God's word through His prophet, she received the reward of obedience, which was life instead of death, and sufficiency instead of lack.

God told Elijah that He had commanded a widow woman to feed him. But when he found the woman at the gate of Zarephath, she didn't know anything about what God told Elijah. But she received Elijah's word all the same, and it meant the difference between daily bread and certain death. She went to the gate looking for sticks that would cook food for one day—perhaps her last meal on earth. But instead she found a word that sustained her, her son, and Elijah for the remainder of the crisis. If she had not obeyed God, she would have starved, her son would have starved, and barring some other miraculous intervention, Elijah would have starved.

Here is a nugget of truth you need to guard like gold—when a word from God is given, reason is never required—faith and faith alone must answer the door.

The widow had not heard from God until she heard from the prophet of God. If she had tried to determine her response to that word through her mental reasoning, she would have thought Elijah was just a beggar like so many others she had seen through the lean years. Past experience would have suggested that she pay no attention to the stranger at the gate. But faith stepped in and persuaded her that there was something better for her, and she obeyed the prophet's request. Her seed planted into his life resulted in a harvest that outlasted the famine.

She gave her last cake to the prophet, and God gave her a life-saving harvest. One meager meal for one, which was the best she had to offer, was multiplied into many meals that satisfied three through the rest of the season of famine.

This miracle of multiplication reminds me of the time when Jesus provided for the multitude that gathered to hear him teach in the region around Galilee. He provided food for all of them as the result of one boy giving his lunch of loaves and fishes. A small seed given in faith can result in extraordinary abundance when we place it in the hands of God.

The reason many in the church are not prospering is because they have not regarded the word of the man or woman of God as the word of the Lord. They have to try to determine for themselves whether or not God is speaking to them, and through whom. If the widow had waited to check out Elijah's resume, she would have starved to death.

Certainly we must be discriminating and recognize that not everyone has the word of the Lord in them. There were false prophets then as well as now. But God sent Elijah to the widow not with the purpose of taking something from her, but to give something to her that she could never have produced on her own. If she refused to obey, she would not be the only one to suffer.

The Bible does not say that her meal barrel became full and her cruse of oil overflowed. I don't believe that is the way it happened. This passage indicates to me that every day when the woman went to check the barrel, there was enough in it for that day, and the same with the oil. The woman had to exercise her faith every day for provision, and her faith was rewarded.

Jesus taught His disciples to pray, "Give us this day our daily bread...." God is pleased when we trust Him, not in uncertain riches laid up where moths and rust can corrupt it or thieves can break through and steal it.

When Israel passed through the wilderness on their way to the Promised Land, God sent manna from heaven six days a week, as well as meat in the form of quail. But this provision was made daily, except for the Sabbath. God didn't give them a six month supply all at once. He required them to trust Him every day for provision. They couldn't carry more than a day's supply with them on their travels anyway.

I'm not saying you can't have a savings account—but I am saying we must trust God every day, and not just when things are difficult for us economically and it looks as though there is no other way. God never condemns wealth, but He does warn against putting our trust in riches instead of in Him. The widow in this story didn't need a bag of gold—there was no meal in the marketplace for any price. What she needed was enough oil and meal to provide for her household and that is what God provided through her obedience.

God has not forgotten about you, regardless of how desperate your situation has become. Things may be so bad that the only plan that makes sense to you is to eat whatever remains and die. That was the widow's plan before the prophet met her at the gate. Whatever your plan may be, God has a different plan—a better plan. Jeremiah chapter 29 verse 11 says: "For I know the thoughts that I think toward you, saith the Lord, thoughts of peace, and not of evil, to give you an expected end."

When God asks you for something, it is never because He wants to decrease you, but because He intends to increase you. What is in His hand is always bigger than what is in your hand; but you cannot receive what is in His hand until you release what is in your hand. You can never accept what He has for you while you are holding on to what you already have.

When the widow offered her cake to Elijah, she was giving the seed that was in her hand to God by giving it to God's representative. God multiplied her seed and produced a harvest that blessed others as well as the widow herself.

God wants to use you to be a blessing to others. It is not difficult to become introverted and think exclusively in terms of my needs, my concerns and my desires. God is interested in our blessing, but He wants our focus to become outward instead of inward. The woman was only thinking of herself and her son in her extremity. Elijah's presence and his demand made her think of someone besides herself. When she opened her life to someone outside of her circle, she opened herself to be both a recipient and a channel of God's miraculous provision.

What would happen in our families, our churches, and our communities if we would adopt the same attitude? Our little could become much if we put it in God's loving hands. What if, instead of bickering over where we were going to eat, we put some of what we had into a bag or a box and delivered it to a family that had nothing? Not only would they be blessed, but God would multiply what remained, making sure that there was no lack in our lives. If doing this personally is more than you can manage, at least support a ministry effort that feeds hungry people at your church or in your community. God will bless you to be a blessing to others if you will allow Him to by your willingness to give.

Before we leave the story of the widow of Zarephath, there is one more thing I want to point out. If we are not careful, Bible narratives can seem like fairy tales with everyone living happily ever after. Of course you know that life very seldom fits into that category.

The woman and her son survived the famine as a result of miraculous intervention. But just because they made it through that difficult time didn't mean they wouldn't ever experience any more adversity.

The children of Israel escaped the bondage of Egypt only to face a wilderness where there was no water. Jacob departed from his dishonest father-in-law, but then had to face his estranged brother Esau. Paul survived the shipwreck but was bitten by a serpent. Life is full of challenges, and we cannot quit believing God just because we have experienced a great victory.

No doubt you have experienced this as well. You get your car fixed and your roof starts to leak. You repay a debt for one unexpected expense and another comes up. You get a raise at work but then your utility bills increase. But before you throw up your hands in despair, listen to what happened to the widow.

After the famine was broken and rain returned to Israel, the widow's son died. This was particularly tragic, since he had been rescued from the jaws of death by starvation just a short time before. But the widow did not accept his death as final. She went to Elijah, who took the matter to the Lord. God told him to stretch himself out over the boy three times. Elijah did so, and God brought the boy back from the dead.

If you have seed in the ground, your harvest can come back to you in many different forms. Just because you eat and are satisfied as the result of a seed you sow doesn't mean that God's power of multiplication has been exhausted. In this case, the woman placed a demand upon the same ministry gift she had sown into just a short time before. She didn't realize it, but her seed went into her future and produced a harvest for her that she didn't even know she would need. The result was her son's resurrection from the dead.

Think about the dreams that are dormant within you. Call to remembrance all the great things that you have determined to do for God. Regardless of how impossible it looks, plant a seed in faith and watch God resurrect that thing and place it in your arms again.

Our God is supernatural,
and He will go beyond the ordinary
to get us what we need.

CHAPTER FOUR
BEARING FRUIT IN THE MIDDLE OF WINTER

There was snow on the mountains around Jerusalem on that midwinter day. It was unusually cold, and the wind made it feel even colder. But the snow was not the only thing that was shining white in the sunlight. The almond trees were in bloom, and their delicate white petals looked like snowdrops that stopped and stayed on the tree limbs instead of falling to the ground. It was always a stirring sight—instead of green shoots and sprouting buds that were the common signs of spring, the almonds bloomed before buds or leaves came out. It was just the white blossoms that stood out in contrast to the bare limbs in the barrenness of winter.

Jeremiah was taking all this in when the Lord spoke to him: "Jeremiah, what seest thou?"

He immediately replied, "I see a rod of an almond tree."

The Lord said, "Thou hast well seen: for I will hasten my word to perform it."

In ancient Israel, the almond tree was a harbinger of change. Their petite white blossoms were the first sign in the midst of the harsh winds and cold rains of winter that hope was still alive, and that soon the air would be warm and the earth ready to bring forth its abundance. God promised the prophet that His word would come to pass just as He had spoken it.

It is a wonderful thing to travel down the country lanes around my home in autumn and see apple orchards full of fruit. The combination of reds, golds, and greens is truly breathtaking. If the harvest is particularly bountiful, you can even smell the scent of apples in the air.

As remarkable as all this is, it would even be more noteworthy if you would travel down those same roads in the middle of winter and see an apple tree in the middle of the orchard bearing fruit with snow all around. It would certainly attract everyone's attention, with good reason. It would be both supernatural and spectacular.

God spoke to me about this passage one day in January. He said to me, "I want you to blossom and bear fruit in the middle of winter."

When I think of the middle of winter, I automatically think of my birthday. I was born on January 13, in St. Luke's Hospital in Cuyahoga County, Ohio, and there was 22 inches of snow on the ground. People who have heard me say this often ask if there was really that much snow there that day. My family has a picture of my uncle sitting on a bench outside the hospital the day I was born with the snow on either side of him nearly level with his shoulders. You can't get much more in the middle of winter than that!

How can we bear fruit in the middle of winter? After all, winter is a time for rest and dormancy, in preparation for the activity and renewal that comes with spring. Yet, God told Jeremiah that He would hasten His word to perform it, meaning that His word was powerful enough that it could produce at any time, regardless of the date on the calendar. Even though we see examples of spiritual truths in natural things, God is by no means limited to natural seasons to accomplish His purposes.

Since Israel was primarily an agricultural society, God used many natural illustrations to teach them about Himself. Much of Jesus' teaching was in terms that farmers and fishermen could easily understand. But just because these natural processes are good examples of spiritual things does not mean that God is constrained by them. Our God is supernatural, and will go beyond the ordinary to get us what we need. Even though we are natural people and subject to some natural limitations, when it comes to God, we need to take the limits off.

Let me explain by using Isaiah chapter 55 as an example of the omnipotence and omniscience of a transcendent and triumphant God. Verses 9-11 contain the essence:

> For as the heavens are higher than the earth, so are my ways higher than your ways, and my thoughts than your thoughts. For as the rain cometh down, and the snow from heaven, and re-

> turneth not thither, but watereth the
> earth, and maketh it bring forth and bud,
> that it may give seed to the sower, and
> bread to the eater: so shall my word be
> that goeth forth out of my mouth: it shall
> not return unto me void, but it shall ac-
> complish that which I please, and it
> shall prosper in the thing whereto I sent
> it.

There is a tremendously important paradox
contained in these few verses that has everything to do with your giving and your faith.

Of course, it is not difficult at all to recognize that God's thoughts are higher than ours,
and that His ways are higher than ours. This is
so evident that I won't take time to elaborate on
it here.

God goes on through His prophet Isaiah to
explain that He sends rain and snow from
heaven to water the earth. We are familiar with
the natural process that explains how precipita-
tion falls to the ground, replenishes the earth,
and then through evaporation rises again into
the atmosphere as water vapor to fall once again
as rain or snow. It is a fascinating process, and

takes place naturally as a result of natural forces that God set in motion at creation.

But God did not stop at describing a natural process. He goes on to say that in the same way that the rain and snow fall from heaven, His word comes from heaven to bless the earth. Just as natural rain causes growth and multiplication of natural seed sown in the earth, the Word causes spiritual growth and multiplication. But notice that God says the rain comes from heaven, but doesn't come back again (at least, not as rain). Later in the passage, however, God says His word shall not return to Him void, or empty, but filled with power to accomplish His will.

Here is the question: how is God's Word going to return to Him from the earth? He sends it from heaven, and very clearly says it will not come back to Him void. But how?

From the natural example of rainfall and evaporation, we see that the Word has to get back to heaven somehow. But what process has to take place to make it happen?

Psalm 103:20 gives us a clue. "Bless the Lord, ye his angels, that excel in strength, that do his commandments, hearkening unto the voice of his word."

The Bible says the angels listen to the voice of the word. Someone has to give a voice to the word of God in order to send it back into the heavens to accomplish God's purpose. That someone has to be on the earth, not in heaven, and they have to be able to speak to give voice to the word of God.

That someone is you and me.

In order for God's Word to accomplish all that He pleases and prosper in the thing He has sent it to do, someone needs to give it a voice. It has no voice of its own—someone on the earth must pick it up and speak it in faith in order for it to have its desired effect. This is the way God intends for His Word to come back to Him, filled with power to do what He has sent it to do. If it is not spoken, it lies dormant like seed that has not yet been planted in fertile soil.

God said the rain causes the earth to produce both seed and bread. In the same way, the Word of God sent from heaven will cause you to have not only seed to sow but bread to eat. The apostle Paul echoed this thought in 2 Corinthians 9:10 when he said,

> Now he that ministereth seed to the sower both minister bread for your food, and multiply your seed sown, and increase the fruits of your righteousness.

But one very important stipulation in Isaiah 55 is that we must send God's Word back to Him in heaven by giving it a voice—by speaking it in faith.

Here is an example. The Bible says in Ephesians 5:1 (NIV) that we should be imitators of God, as children imitate their parents. Anyone who has ever watched children know that they are great imitators. They mimic the expressions, the words, and the attitudes of those they respect.

We are children of God, so we ought to imitate the behaviors of our heavenly Father. In order to do that, we need to spend time with Him so we know how He acts. We need to spend time in His Word so we know what He has said. We need to become familiar with the life and ministry of Jesus, because Jesus said if we wanted to know what the Father was like, all we had to do was look at Him.

So how does God act? Let's look at the very beginning of human history, starting in Genesis. In the very first chapter, God speaks ten different times and remarkable creativity flows forth as a result of His words. He repeats the creative process to the point of monotony—and every time He says something, it happens just as He says it.

God's creative acts culminate with the creation of Adam and his wife, and then something else remarkable happens—God gives them authority to do what He has done up to that time. Adam and Eve begin to rule and reign under God using the authority He gave them, and that authority was wrapped up in the words they spoke.

Think of it this way—the root of the word *authority* is *author*—one who deals in words. Adam and Eve exercised authority as a result of the words they used. No other category of created being had the authority that they had. They used words just like they had seen God use words, and whatever they said happened. They literally imitated God, and God was pleased with the result. This continued until deception and sin entered the picture through the fall of Adam and Eve.

Now, because of the redemptive work of Jesus, we have been returned to the original state of affairs in terms of our authority. As redeemed people, we have the ability and the opportunity to rule and reign under God the same way Adam did. But in order to do so, we must also imitate God as Adam did—that is, we must speak the words God sent from heaven and return them to Him from the earth. We must say what God says, and believe it when we say it. As we do, His word will not return void, but will accomplish the things He sent it to do.

What has this to do with your sowing and reaping a harvest? Here's an illustration from Deuteronomy 26:3-11. Moses commanded the children of Israel to follow some specific instructions when they came into their land of promise. Included in these instructions were what they needed to say when they brought their tithe to the Lord.

> And thou shalt go unto the priest that shall be in those days, and say unto him, I profess this day unto the Lord thy God, that I am come unto the country which the Lord sware unto our fathers for to give us. And the priest shall take the basket out of thine hand, and set it down before the altar of the Lord thy God.

> And thou shalt speak and say before the Lord thy God, A Syrian ready to perish was my father, and he went down into Egypt, and sojourned there with a few, and became there a nation, great, mighty, and populous: and the Egyptians evil entreated us, and afflicted us, and laid upon us hard bondage: and when we cried unto the Lord God of our fathers, the Lord heard our voice, and looked on our affliction, and our labour,

and our oppression: and the Lord brought us forth out of Egypt with a mighty hand, and with an outstretched arm, and with great terribleness, and with signs, and with wonders: and he hath brought us into this place, and hath given us this land, even a land that floweth with milk and honey.

And now, behold, I have brought the firstfruits of the land, which thou, O Lord, hast given me. And thou shalt set it before the Lord thy God, and worship before the Lord thy God: and thou shalt rejoice in every good thing which the Lord thy God hath given unto thee, and unto thine house, thou, and the Levite, and the stranger that is among you.

Don't let the cultural things in this passage such as putting your tithe in a basket and taking it to a human priest trouble you. The thing I want you to see is that the worshippers were commanded to say some things when they brought their tithe to the Lord. One of the things they were supposed to rehearse was how God brought them out of a land of bondage and into a land of blessing. They were commanded never to forget the grace and glory of God that delivered them from a lifetime of servitude.

It would be a good idea for us to do the same when we bring our tithes into the storehouse. God has been good to us, and we need to remind ourselves of His goodness. If we would do so, it would help keep us from complaining so much, since we would have a chance to remember how bad it was before God set us free.

Next, they were to thank God for the tithe they had to place before Him. They would not have had it if God had not given it to them, and it was only right that they should be thankful.

We could use more thankfulness in the body of Christ, since some people think they got everything they have as a result of their own effort. What we had before we met God was death, and we should be thankful every day for every benefit we have received by His grace.

Finally, God's people were commanded to worship and rejoice as they brought their tithes and offerings to Him. Giving is an act of worship.

This is hard for some people to understand, so let me try to help you understand. When you work, you are essentially exchanging your time and effort, the sweat of your brow, the brawn of your back, and the thoughts of your brain for money. That's what your employer gives you in exchange for your life. So we could say that money represents your life.

When we bring our seed to the Lord, we are not just throwing some money in an offering plate—we are giving God what represents a portion of our lives. We should do it humbly and reverently, but also joyfully, because without God's blessing on our lives, there would be no way we would have the strength or the knowledge or the ability to work.

When we express our thanksgiving and praise to God as we bring our offerings to Him, we are literally returning His word to the heavenlies as He instructed us to do in Isaiah chapter 55. He assured us that His word would not return void, but that it would accomplish what He pleased and would prosper in the thing that He sent it forth to do.

Many years ago, as I was asking God about finances, He said to me, "You haven't been tithing." This came as quite a shock to me, because as far as I knew, I had tithed every dollar I had from the time I got saved when I was eight years old.

"But God," I protested, "I have been tithing. I've been a tither all my life."

God directed me to Deuteronomy 26, and said, "You've been putting money in the plate, but you haven't been tithing." I saw it then—the quality of the words I spoke over my seed was just as important as the seed itself. By rehearsing my condition before God found me, and by thanking God for what He had given me, and by rejoicing in what He had enabled me to sow back into His kingdom, I was literally sowing the heavens with the Word of God, and causing the power of that Word to be released over my seed, my field, and my life.

This is a principle that will help us any time we sow a seed into the kingdom of God, but I have found that it is especially important to do this when things have become tight financially. As we honor God by returning His Word to Him, we will become like those almond branches blooming before anything else has budded. We will be like an apple tree flourishing and bearing fruit in the middle of winter. We are sure to attract the attention of God as we do, and His blessing will surely abide upon us.

If you have encountered financial difficulty, don't withhold anything from God. Say what He has said about your finances and about your life. Keep on speaking, regardless of what you see. The Bible assures us that His Word will not return to Him void. God takes pleasure in the prosperity of His servants, and He will take pleasure in increasing you.

And David said,
"Is there yet any that is left
of the house of Saul,
that I may shew him kindness
for Jonathan's sake?"

CHAPTER FIVE
A COVENANT OF PROVISION

A feeling of dread filled the atmosphere as the army of Israel moved to block a far superior force of Philistines that threatened the very center of the country. Samuel the prophet was dead, and rumors of King Saul's instability had been circulating for some time. Nobody could tell for sure what the outcome of the battle would be, but hearts were heavy and countenances at the court were lined with worry.

Finally the battle was joined, and everyone's worst fears were confirmed. The Philistines' assault shattered the demoralized defenders, and soon a full fledged rout was under way. Israel lay prostrate before the invaders. In the panic that followed, those of Saul's household fled to the other side of the Jordan River, fearful that the Philistines would seek to kill all the members of the royal family.

As one of the nurses was making her escape with one of Saul's grandchildren, she fell in her haste and dropped the boy. He landed heavily, and began to scream in pain. There was no time to tend his injuries, and even though he was seriously hurt, there was little she could do except hold him tight as she followed the other exiles to a place of relative safety. Everything was noise and confusion, and there was little thought given to anything except survival. The leadership of Israel was either dead or scattered, and the fugitives had to make do with whatever accommodations they could find. Many of them settled in remote places where their identity was unknown, and where they could hope against hope for a change of fortune.

A few generations before, Israel crossed the Jordan after their wilderness adventure and possessed the Promised Land. After Joshua died, God raised up judges to rule the land. Freedom and servitude came in alternating parts depending on whether or not the leadership trusted God or not. Eventually Israel demanded a king, and God told Samuel to anoint Saul, the son of Kish to go forth and lead Israel in her battles. At first, Saul did well, but as his reign continued he became paranoid and obsessed with consolidating his throne against imaginary enemies. He became crueler and more calculating as the years went by, and was deeply suspicious of those around him. It was in the midst of these circumstances that two of the men who loved Saul most and served him best befriended one another.

First Samuel chapter 20 tells the story of David and Jonathan. At first glance, it would seem odd that these two men would develop anything but a rivalry. Jonathan was the son of Saul, and was next in line of succession to be king, and David was the favorite of all Israel after his victory over Goliath, the Philistine giant. It is a testament to the character of both of them that they had a friendship that led to them making a covenant with one another, as we see in verse 42:

> And Jonathan said to David, Go in peace, forasmuch as we have sworn both of us in the name of the Lord, saying, The Lord be between me and thee, and between my seed and thy seed for

ever. And he arose and departed: and
Jonathan went into the city.

David became a fugitive from the wrath of
Saul, and never saw his covenant brother Jonathan again except for one brief meeting while
David was in exile, where they confirmed the
agreement they had with one another.

Saul's obsession with trying to kill David
caused him to neglect his responsibilities to se-
cure his borders, and soon the Philistines over-
ran his outnumbered army. Saul and Jonathan
were both slain on the slopes of Mount Gilboa,
and for a time it appeared that the Philistines
would destroy the entire nation of Israel. A long
period of upheaval followed, but eventually
David ascended to the throne of all Israel. Hope
once again flourished that Israel would become
a great nation.

David's first order of business was securing
his borders from the deprivations of the Philistines, who were relentless in their determination
to wreak havoc on the rebuilding country and
her new king. But God was with David and

gave him victory over his enemies on every hand. David then brought the ark of the covenant to Jerusalem and dealt with some border clashes with his other enemies. Finally, there was peace, both within the nation and with the neighboring countries. God then reminded David of a solemn promise he had made many years before. We find the story in 2 Samuel, chapter 9, verses 1-4:

> And David said, Is there yet any that is left of the house of Saul, that I may shew him kindness for Jonathan's sake? And there was of the house of Saul a servant whose name was Ziba. And when they had called him unto David, the king said unto him, Art thou Ziba? And he said, Thy servant is he. And the king said, Is there not yet any of the house of Saul, that I may shew the kindness of God unto him? And Ziba said unto the king, Jonathan hath yet a son, which is lame on his feet. And the king said unto him, Where is he? And Ziba said unto the king, Behold, he is in the house of Machir, the son of Ammiel, in Lo-debar.

David had not forgotten his covenant with Jonathan that they had solemnly sworn so long ago. Even though Jonathan was dead, David's commitment did not end the day Jonathan lost his life at the hand of an uncircumcised Philistine. His covenant with Jonathan extended to his descendants as well. David was far removed from the events that took place on Mount Gilboa on that fateful day, and so had to inquire about the status of Saul's household.

He found a forgotten servant named Ziba who had some valuable information. He informed the king that Jonathan had a surviving son named Mephibosheth, who was lame, and was dwelling in a place called Lo-debar.

Remember, Mephibosheth was the same person who as a child was injured and became lame. For many years he had lived in a wilderness, far from the centers of civilization and culture. A crisis in the nation became a catastrophe for him. He would have been raised in a position of privilege, and may have even been heir to the throne, but instead was dwelling in Lo-debar, which means "no pasture."

Mephibosheth was born to royalty, yet had little or nothing he could call his own. During the time of his exile he had an inheritance that he could not enjoy because of events over which he had no control. He was a member of a once prominent and respected family, but was now living like a fugitive, far from the favor and blessing that had been his. Adding to all this, he was lame in his feet, and was severely limited in what he could do for himself. Virtually every occupation he could have pursued to help himself was closed to him, which made him dependent on others for his very existence.

Think of the resentment that must have brooded in his heart. Instead of living in the courts of favor and fame, he was relegated to a hut in a one horse town in the wilderness. Instead of being at the center of power, he was on the fringes of civilization. Instead of being capable and courageous, he was alone and ashamed. Instead of having a future and a fortune, he had fear and failure. His was an existence of squalor, not splendor. He became accustomed to being satisfied with the crumbs that fell from someone else's table. Every day was a burden.

Even though he was far removed from the notable events taking place on the other side of Jordan, eventually news came to him that David had ascended to the throne of Israel—the throne that could have been his. His heart was divided when he heard the news. On one hand, he was tempted to become angry at the misfortune that had befallen him and kept him from occupying his rightful station in life. He wanted to hate David and blame him for his condition, but he realized that was foolishness—David had nothing to do with why he was where he was. As time went on, Mephibosheth realized that nobody would want a castoff cripple such as him to be their leader. The doors to wealth, prestige, and honor were all closed to him. He would never be any more than he was—a hopeless case on the borders of humanity.

A much more real dilemma was that David would find out about him and hunt him down like an animal. After all, wasn't it customary for kings to try to eliminate all their potential competition? Maybe there was an advantage to his life in the obscurity of the wilderness after all. As the years passed, the flame of anger and resentment flickered, and finally went out, replaced by a foreboding about the future. It became harder and harder for him to find a reason to continue his miserable existence far below the privileges that had eluded him for so long.

One day shortly after he arose, Mephibosheth saw a cloud of dust in the distance. It would take a long column of travelers to make such a disturbance, and nobody ever came to Lo-debar. As he wondered who it could be, fear gripped his heart. David the king had found out about him, and had sent his army to come and kill him!

Even though he had often contemplated death, when it finally became real to him, Mephibosheth realized how much he wanted to live. So many dreams, so many plans, so many things not done! He thought about running, but he was lame—there was no way he could avoid capture that way. Besides, where could he go?

Fighting was out of the question. He barely had the strength to perform the most basic of tasks. It was ludicrous to think of resisting the trained soldiers of the king.

As the horsemen at the head of the column came into view, Mephibosheth struggled to hide himself under the table in his little hut. He dragged his crippled feet as far back as he could and made himself as small as possible. He pulled the table cover down in front of him and waited, shivering in fear.

Soon there were footsteps outside his door. Someone announced the servants of King David. Then the door opened, and several men crossed the threshold. In a few moments they searched the small space that was Mephibosheth's home and found him cowering under the table. Strong arms pulled him from his hiding place and set him on a horse for the trip back to Jerusalem. They left everything he had ever known behind, taking only his crutches with him. For Mephibosheth, it was a frightening trip into an uncertain future.

Let's pick up the narrative again from our text in 2 Samuel 9: 6-11:

> Now when Mephibosheth, the son of Jonathan, the son of Saul, was come unto David, he fell on his face, and did reverence. And David said, Mephibosheth. And he answered, Behold thy servant! And David said unto him, Fear not: for I will surely shew thee kindness for Jonathan thy father's sake, and will restore thee all the land of Saul thy father; and thou shalt eat bread at my table continually.

> And he bowed himself, and said, What is thy servant, that thou shouldest look upon such a dead dog as I am?

> Then the king called to Ziba, Saul's servant, and said unto him, I have given unto thy master's son all that pertained to Saul and to all his house. Thou therefore, and thy sons, and thy servants, shall till the land for him, and thou shalt bring in the fruits, that thy master's son may have food to eat: but Mephibosheth thy master's son shall eat bread alway at my table. Now Ziba had fifteen sons and

twenty servants. Then said Ziba unto the king, According to all that my lord the king hath commanded his servant, so shall thy servant do. As for Mephibosheth, said the king, he shall eat at my table, as one of the king's sons.

When Mephibosheth came into David's presence, he fell prostrate and awaited the king's judgment. He had heard stories about David's complete and total victory over all his enemies, and he expected death, or at least harsh punishment. He even referred to himself as a dead dog, which in those days was about as contemptible a descriptive expression as a person could use.

It is hard for us to imagine what Mephibosheth must have thought upon hearing what David said. No doubt it was hard for him to believe. Instead of certain death, he had just been given everything that had been taken from his family many years before. In addition, he had an entire cadre of servants who would work his fields and do his bidding. But best of all, David had just awarded him a place at the royal table—he said Mephibosheth would be given the same privileges and provision as one of the king's sons. He had gone from obscurity to royalty in one day. It was hard to take it all in.

Soon afterward, servants whisked him away to private quarters where he could bathe and change into royal robes that were provided for him. The old sticks padded with rags that were so familiar as his crutches were taken away and replaced by new ones that were beautifully crafted. His crippled feet were banded with customized leather sandals. His hair was combed and his beard trimmed. Then he was summoned to the king's table to eat with all the rest of the royal family. It was as though his life had started over.

After he was seated and before the king came in, he overheard some of the servants whispering about him. "Who is that little crippled man? Who does he think he is, sitting at the king's table as one of the king's sons? He doesn't deserve to be here!"

In a rush, all the feelings of hopelessness and helplessness he had before threatened to overwhelm Mephibosheth. The servants were absolutely correct. He didn't deserve to be here. Who did he think he was, putting on airs and acting as though he was one of the king's sons? Despair shot through him, and he nearly got out of his seat to bolt for the nearest door. Then he remembered something that David said to him.

"Don't be afraid," the king had said. "I will show kindness to you for your father Jonathan's sake." When David reached for Mephibosheth's prostrate form, Mephibosheth saw a mark on David's wrist. He thought it was a scar from one of the many battles he had been through, but it dawned on him that it may not have been a wound that came because of conflict, but a mark of love and loyalty and trust. He remembered the word covenant meant to cut.

"For your father Jonathan's sake..." Mephibosheth had never really known his father Jonathan. He died in battle when Mephibosheth was very young. But something happened between Jonathan and David, something that was stronger than death—something that made a difference, not just to the two men that were directly involved, but to all their descendants.

A covenant. Jonathan and David made a covenant with one another. It must have happened even before Mephibosheth was born. Even though Jonathan died, David was now fulfilling the terms of the covenant he had made many years ago, and as Jonathan's son, Mephibosheth was the recipient of the blessings of that covenant.

He turned to the servants who had been whispering about him. He declared, "You're absolutely right. I have no right to be here. Nothing I have done or could ever do could qualify me to sit at the king's table as one of his sons. But when King David arrives, I want you to notice that mark on his wrist. That is the sign of a covenant that he made with my father Jonathan. The king is a covenant keeper, and that is what gives me the right to be here. Now hush your foolish talking before you are found speaking against a covenant partner of the king."

I don't know of a story that better illustrates the situation we were in before we accepted Jesus as our Savior. Paul explains our hopeless state in these words from Ephesians 2:12:

> That at that time ye were without Christ, being aliens from the commonwealth of Israel, and strangers from the covenants of promise, having no hope, and without God in the world.

That describes all of us—we were without Christ, without God, strangers from the covenants of promise, and had no hope. But thank God, He didn't leave us there.

Verse 13 goes on to say: "But now in Christ Jesus ye who sometimes were far off are made nigh by the blood of Christ." We are now partakers of a covenant from which we were formerly estranged. That covenant is a covenant of supernatural provision.

Mephibosheth had nothing to offer David in return for his generosity. But he didn't need to offer anything but himself. The covenant did not depend on Mephibosheth's lack; it depended on David's abundance. In fact, the covenant wasn't with Mephibosheth, it was with his father Jonathan—but all Jonathan's descendants were included.

God made a covenant with Jesus Christ, who represented all humanity. When we are born again, we become members of God's family and partakers of the covenant. As a believer, you have the privilege of partaking of all that the King has to offer—and it has nothing to do with what you have or don't have. I like to say it this way: crippled feet are no bar to sonship. In fact, under a king's table is a good place to hide your infirmity.

You have been summoned from your place in Lo-debar into the presence of the King so He can lavish His blessings upon you. He wants to restore everything that has been stolen from you. I encourage you to partake of the covenant of provision that God made long before you were born.

But thou shalt remember
the LORD thy God:
for it is he that giveth thee
power to get wealth,
that he may establish his covenant
which he sware unto thy fathers,
as it is this day.
~Deuteronomy 8:18

CHAPTER SIX
THE GOD OF MORE THAN ENOUGH

They had run out of water. What had seemed like a simple enough campaign at the beginning had turned into a trap, and drought and death would devastate them before they ever faced their enemies. In seven days of marching they had not found one oasis, and there was not enough water remaining among the troops to get back to a reliable water source. Unrest ran through the ranks while the leaders huddled to try to come up with a plan.

Soon the word came back through the chain of command, and everyone who could hold a shovel was ordered to start digging.

"I don't see what use it is trying to dig a well in this wilderness," one soldier grumbled to another.

"We're not digging wells, we're digging ditches," said his companion.

"Ditches? That's even more ridiculous. What do we need ditches for? There's no water to put in them! Whoever heard of such a thing?"

"Save your breath and keep digging," came the reply.

The occasion of this soldier's discontent was a military campaign by the kings of Israel, Judah, and Edom against the rebellious kingdom of Moab. Their way led them through the barren desert, and they found no water there to sustain them. Before they gave up in despair, Jehoshaphat, king of Judah, asked if there was a prophet among them of whom they could inquire. Elisha was nearby, so the kings went to him for counsel.

His answer is found in 2 Kings 3:16-17:

> And he said, Thus saith the Lord, Make this valley full of ditches. For thus saith the Lord, Ye shall not see wind, neither shall ye see rain; yet that valley shall be filled with water, that ye may drink, both ye, and your cattle, and your beasts.

The kings did not argue with this word, regardless of how ridiculous it sounded. They immediately ordered their men to fill the valley with ditches. The day grew long and dust covered the encampment, but there was still no relief in sight. By nightfall, it seemed as though their goal was further away than ever before.

But in the morning, the three allied armies awoke to a sign and a wonder: the valley they had scored with trenches the previous day was filled with water. There had been neither wind nor rain during the night, but the God of Elisha the prophet had performed a miracle and given them more life-sustaining water then they could possibly use. Everyone drank their fill, and God gave them victory over their enemies as well.

The soldiers whose hands were cracked and blistered from digging in the parched earth were glad that they did as they were told despite how strange their orders were.

I was meditating on this passage years ago when God spoke to me very distinctly. He said, "If you want to see miracles, dig a ditch—prepare for increase." As I put this into practice in my life, God proved to me again that He is always a God of more than enough. But without obedience, no word from God will be effective.

A favorite pastime of many Christians is arguing with God in an effort to determine why He wants them to do a certain thing. I have discovered that this is a colossal waste of time. God is not obligated to tell you the reason for anything He does. God is sovereign, and does things far beyond our ability to understand. This doesn't mean we should not use our God-given ability to think and to reason, but when it comes to obeying His commands, we are far better off to just obey without hesitation and without reservation.

God gave Jeremiah an object lesson in submitting to His will at the potter's house. We find the story in Jeremiah 18:1-6:

> The word which came to Jeremiah from the Lord, saying, Arise, and go down to the potter's house, and there I will cause thee to hear my words. Then I went down to the potter's house, and, behold, he wrought a work on the wheels. And the vessel that he made of clay was marred in the hand of the potter: so he made it again another vessel, as seemed good to the potter to make it.

> Then the word of the Lord came to me,
> saying, O house of Israel, cannot I do
> with you as this potter? saith the Lord.
> Behold, as the clay is in the potter's
> hand, so are ye in mine hand, O house
> of Israel.

The message was clear. God is the potter,
and we are the clay. Just as the potter can fashion anything he wants from the lump of clay,
which has neither form nor function before the
potter puts his hand upon it, so God can make
us into a vessel fit for any use, and require any
function He desires from us.

Paul echoes this idea in Romans 9:20:

> Nay but, O man, who art thou that
> repliest against God? Shall the thing
> formed say to him that formed it, Why
> hast thou made me thus?

We can see the foolishness of trying to require from God the reasons that He asks us to
do anything. We should rather say, "Yes, Lord!"
Many times the reasons will become clear to us
only after we have obeyed.

When Elisha prophesied about ditches in the valley, God's intention was to provide water for the army that was assembled there. None of the soldiers would have guessed how God could have done it, but their obedience literally saved their lives. If there had been no ditches in the valley, God could have sent a flood, but it would have been wasted, because there would have been nothing to hold the water He sent.

We say we want increase, but many times our actions belie our words, because we make no preparations for the increase we say we desire.

If you want revelation from God, stop watching so much television or spending so much time on the Internet. If you need friends, get out of your house and get around other people. If you want your finances to increase, arrange for a place to put the money you expect to have. If you are looking forward to an evening meal at a fine restaurant, it makes no sense to spend all afternoon snacking on junk food.

Make sure there is room for what you say you want God to give you.

Then too, you must intentionally move something out of the way to make a place for what you want to acquire. If you get new furniture, you can't just put it on top of what you already have. You have to move out the old to make room for the new. I know of families who have what they call the garage sale rule: they can't bring something else in their house until something of equal size goes out. There simply isn't room for everything we think we need to keep.

It is not enough for us to just layer in a new way of thinking on top of the old ways that have resulted in never having enough. We must move out the old ways to make space for the fullness that God wants to give us.

You may be familiar with an old saying that goes like this: "He's penny wise but pound foolish." It means some people will spend more trying to save a few cents than it is worth. Some folks will burn ten dollars' worth of gasoline to go to a station where they can save a few cents a gallon. When all is said and done, they have lost more than they gained.

Our obedience is worth more than we have realized. We can let go of a little in obedience to God and gain what is much more valuable.

A little boy once put his hand in a vase that had been part of his mother's family for generations. When he tried to pull his hand out, he found that it was stuck. The family did everything they could think of to remove the boy's hand to no avail. They even called the local fire department for their assistance. After much agonizing, the mother decided that as precious as the heirloom was, they would have to break the vase to rescue her son from his predicament. Suddenly, the little boy had an idea. "Mommy," he said, "would it help if I let go of the penny?" He did, and his hand popped out immediately. He knew the value of a penny, but he did not recognize the value of the vase.

Many times what we are holding onto is not nearly as valuable as what God wants to give us, but He cannot place anything in our hands if we are already holding something else. What seems to be a treasure by earthly standards is worth little from heaven's point of view. We need to learn to open our hands to receive what has true value.

Here is another point to consider. We need to stop looking at what we already have as though that is the best God can do for us. Our God is a God of increase. Ephesians 3:20-21 says:

> Now unto him that is able to do exceeding abundantly above all that we ask or think, according to the power that worketh in us, unto him be glory in the church by Christ Jesus throughout all ages, world without end.

Look again at those words "exceeding abundantly above all." That doesn't just mean a little bit beyond, it means far beyond—as far as the heavens are above the earth. And it goes even further—it says above all we ask or think. That tells me that regardless of how outrageous your imagination, God is prepared to do even bigger things on your behalf. The purpose of all this is not so we can become lifted up in pride and think that we did it all ourselves, but to give glory to God forever, and let others see how good God is through the provision and blessing He has brought into our lives.

I want to encourage you to stop looking at what you have as though it were the best God can do for you. It may be better than anything you have experienced, but that is just scratching the surface of God's ability to bless you. Refuse to continue in that "not enough" mentality that has dogged your tracks all your life, and receive a "more than enough" point of view.

Thank God for the place He has given you to live, but take a trip through a neighborhood where you have always wanted to live. Rejoice every time you drive the car God has provided, but stop looking at it as though it were the ultimate in transportation. Go to your bank and open another savings account. It doesn't matter if you don't have much to put in it right now—you're preparing for increase!

Genesis 26 contains another example of this principle in operation. At God's direction, Isaac sojourned in the land of the Philistines during a famine. Verses 12-14 hold the key to this passage:

> Then Isaac sowed in that land, and received in the same year an hundredfold: and the Lord blessed him. And the man waxed great, and went forward, and grew until he became very great: for he had possession of flocks, and possessions of herds, and great store of servants: and the Philistines envied him.

Just as his father Abraham before him, Isaac was a pilgrim in the land of promise. He depended on crops and herds for his livelihood, and could have lost everything during a famine. But he obeyed God's word, and sowed his seed where God told Him, when God told him, even during a famine.

Isaac was an experienced farmer. He knew it wasn't a good idea to expect a harvest during a time of famine, since famines were brought on by drought, and when there was no rain there could be no harvest. But Isaac sowed in obedience to God, and his seed produced an overwhelming harvest in a year with no rain. How could this be? The only answer was that his abundance was the direct result of his obedience to God. Regardless of economic conditions, Isaac became so wealthy the Philistines around him considered him to be a threat. They were envious of his success.

How many times have you heard this: "But times are hard—we're in a recession!" God's economy is not based on how the stock market is doing or how high the price of gold is. When God says plant, we need to plant.

Ecclesiastes 11:4 says, "He that observeth the wind shall not sow; and he that regardeth the clouds shall not reap." There will always be a reason to withhold your seed that makes sense to your natural mind. But there is one sure way never to reap a harvest, and that is if you never plant a seed.

The Philistines were awed by Isaac's abundant harvest in a time of famine. When you plant your seed in obedience to God's Word, the unbelievers around you will take note of your success. The more desperate the economy, consequently, the more attention you will attract. Be sure you give glory to God for your success, and don't try to take the credit yourself. In fact, the reason God blesses with such extravagance is not because He intends His people to hoard up wealth or become wasteful, but so they can use His blessing to be a blessing to others.

There are repeated warnings in the book of Deuteronomy about the dangers of forgetting the God who gives these blessings so liberally. One is in Deuteronomy 6:10-12:

> And it shall be, when the Lord thy God shall have brought thee into the land which he sware unto thy fathers, to Abraham, to Isaac, and to Jacob, to give thee great and goodly cities, which thou buildedst not, and houses full of all good things, which thou filledst not, and wells digged, which thou diggedst not, vineyards and olive trees, which thou plantedst not; when thou shalt have eaten and

be full; then beware lest thou forget the Lord, which brought thee forth out of the land of Egypt, from the house of bondage.

Another is in Deuteronomy 8: 6-14, 18:

Therefore thou shalt keep the commandments of the Lord thy God, to walk in his ways, and to fear him.

For the Lord thy God bringeth thee into a good land, a land of brooks of water, of fountains and depths that spring out of valleys and hills; a land of wheat, and barley, and vines, and fig trees, and pomegranates; a land of oil olive, and honey; a land wherein thou shalt eat bread without scarceness, thou shalt not lack any thing in it; a land whose stones are iron, and out of whose hills thou mayest dig brass.

When thou hast eaten and art full, then thou shalt bless the Lord thy God for the good land which he hath given thee. Beware that thou forget not the Lord thy God, in not keeping his commandments, and his judgments, and his statutes, which I command thee this day: lest when thou hast eaten and art full, and hast built goodly houses, and dwelt therein; and when thy herds and thy flocks multiply, and thy silver and thy gold is multiplied, and all that thou hast is multiplied; then thine heart be lifted up, and thou forget the Lord thy God...

But thou shalt remember the Lord thy God: for it is he that giveth thee power to get wealth, that he may establish his covenant which he sware unto thy fathers, as it is this day.

From these passages and many others throughout the Bible we see that our God is a God of abundance and increase. He takes pleasure in your prosperity, and wants you to enjoy His goodness, not just for yourself, but for those less fortunate around you. In every case, God requires that we remember Him and return thanks to Him for the goodness He has shown us.

Deuteronomy 8:18 is especially important—God wants to give to us in order to establish His covenant in the earth. His purpose in placing good things in our hands is not just so we can live in ease and comfort while others suffer hardship. We must learn to exercise the principles of God's kingdom so we can participate in His abundance and share it with others, along with the good news of salvation through Jesus Christ.

God wants you to be obedient so He can pour out His blessings upon you. He wants you to use these blessings to point other people to Him. We can be most effective in doing so when we have more than enough, instead of never having enough.

When God revealed Himself to Abraham in Genesis 17:1, He referred to Himself as the Almighty God. This literally means "the all sufficient One." Whatever you need, God has it in abundant supply. He is not limited in His ability to supply all you need and more. He is truly the God of more than enough.

Call upon Him in faith so He can answer you. Sow a seed in faith so He can multiply it. Give thanks to Him and allow Him to be the God of more than enough to you.

ABOUT THE AUTHOR

ROD PARSLEY, bestselling author of more than sixty books, is the dynamic pastor of World Harvest Church in Columbus, Ohio, a church with worldwide ministries and a global outreach. As a highly sought-after crusade and conference speaker whom God has raised up as a prophetic voice to America and the world, Parsley is calling people to Jesus Christ through the good news of the Gospel.

In addition to overseeing ten major ministries, he can be seen around the world on the Breakthrough television broadcast, where he proclaims truth from God's Word.

Parsley's refreshingly direct style encourages Christians to examine and eradicate sin from their lives. A fearless champion of living God's way, Parsley follows the high standard set by Jesus Christ and compels his readers to do the same. He and his wife Joni have two children, Ashton and Austin.

OTHER BOOKS BY ROD PARSLEY

Ancient Wells, Living Water

At the Cross, Where Healing Begins

Could It Be?

Culturally Incorrect (NY Times Bestseller)

Don't Look Now

The Day Before Eternity

He Came First

It's Already There – Where Are You?

No Dry Season (Bestseller)

No More Crumbs (Bestseller)

On the Brink (#1 Bestseller)

Preparing for the Glory

Repairers of the Breach

Silent No More

Tribulation to Triumph

What to Do When It's Not Working…Look Again!

For more information about *Breakthrough*,
World Harvest Church, World Harvest Bible College,
Harvest Preparatory School, The Center for Moral Clarity,
or to receive a product list of the many books, CDs, &
DVDs by Rod Parsley, write or call:

BREAKTHROUGH/WORLD HARVEST CHURCH
P.O. Box 32932
Columbus, OH 43232-0932 USA
(614) 837-1990 (Office)
www.RodParsley.com

WORLD HARVEST BIBLE COLLEGE
P.O. Box 32901
Columbus, OH 43232-0901 USA
(614) 837-4088
whbc.RodParsley.com

HARVEST PREPARATORY SCHOOL
P.O. Box 32903
Columbus, OH 43232-0903 USA
(614) 837-1990
hps.RodParsley.com

THE CENTER FOR MORAL CLARITY
P.O. Box 32903
Columbus, OH 43232-9926 USA
(614) 382-1188
cmc.RodParsley.com

For prayer, call the Prayer Center at (800) 424-8644
(Phone lines are open 24 hours a day)